GW01219709

POLITE FORMS

HARRY WHITE

POLITE FORMS

CARYSFORT PRESS

A Carysfort Press Book
Harry White
Polite Forms

First published in Ireland in 2012 as a paperback original by
Carysfort Press, 58 Woodfield, Scholarstown Road
Dublin 16, Ireland

ISBN 978-1-904505-55-6
© Harry White 2012

Typeset by Carysfort Press
Cover design by Brian O'Connor
Printed and bound by eprint limited
Unit 35
Coolmine Industrial Estate
Dublin 15
Ireland

This book is published with the financial assistance of
The Arts Council (An Chomhairle Ealaíon) Dublin, Ireland

Caution: All rights reserved. No part of this book may be printed or reproduced or utilized in any form or by any electronic, mechanical, or other means, now known or hereafter invented including photocopying and recording, or in any information storage or retrieval system without permission in writing from the publishers.

This book is sold subject to the conditions that it shall not, by way of trade or otherwise, be lent, resold, hired out, or otherwise circulated in any form of binding, or cover other than that in which it is published and without a similar condition, including this condition, being imposed on the subsequent purchaser.

For Fiachra and Dara

Contents

Polite Forms	1
The Hairpiece	2
Nana	3
Expedience	4
Box Three, Spool Five	5
Writing	6
Proper Nouns	7
Strictly Private	8
Pray for the Wanderer	9
Vestments	10
Dead Languages	11
AZH 402	12
Bardolino	13
A Musical Life	14
My Remarkable Uncle	15
Something Blue from the Pines	16
Intolerance	17
A War Miniature	18
The Nature of Things	19
The Music Makers	20
The Back Gardens	21
Bucket and Spade	22
The Rider	23
Captain Extra Mild	24
Notices	25
School-Going	26
Junior Infants	27
The Conventions	28

Night Prayers	29
Sunday Mass	30
Radio Sounds	31
Avenues	32
Fathers and Sons	33
In Herbert Park	34
Swimming Lessons	35
Lost Things	36
A Loanword	37
A Farm Visit	38
The Girl in the Frame	39
The Men Who Left	40
Messages	41
Wedding Photos	42
Notes and Acknowledgements	43

POLITE FORMS

Polite Forms

In the sixties, it was always 'Mrs White'
And 'Mrs Lyons' behind the garden walls.
For years, until the hearse, it stayed that way.
Those conversations, lengthening in the halls,
Would deepen into love but never stray
Beyond the married surname. Then one day
My mother called her 'Rachel', just like that,
And 'Sheila', she replied. At once they knew
A girlish repossession of their own,
Distinct from those brisk husbands on the phone
Who frowned at this familiar pride in names,
Or felt the tug of 'liberation' games,
But never saw it coming, soft as air:
The end of married servitude was there.

The Hairpiece

I loved my father, worshipped him, in truth.
He bounded down to breakfast one fine day,
His mouth, his slender hands, his sixties suit,
All as they had been from the start. Dismay
And giggles spread along the table: we
Took in his vanished dome, and in its place
A jet-black, stiff toupée. Then suddenly
He smiled and we all quizzed him, searched his face
For answers. There were none. Week after week,
The reassuring roughness of his cheek
Against my lips in greetings we exchanged
Persuaded me that nothing much had changed.
In all, there were six of us whom he sired:
The hairpiece was removed when he retired.

Nana

Percussive, brisk, a two-step call to order,
A chilly, regal, best-behaviour word,
Nana brooked no grandmaternal nonsense,
No hidden sweets. No refuge was implied.
Instead, it summoned priest-enriched obedience,
Her missal armed with penances and prayers,
Her stern and stylish rectitude; her sense
That being loved came best by being feared.

Other peoples' grandmas were indulgent,
Burbling sloppy promises, never kept,
While Nana ruled in fox furs: groomed, refulgent,
Widowed, vigilant, vehement, correct.

Raised in Chester, she retained through life
An English accent that cut like a knife.

Expedience

In May of 1963, my father
Dashed into town to see his new-born son
While Nana kept us on our toes at home.
We twins were good as gold, but our young brother
Enraged her when he answered back: the one
Unpardonable crime. But there was worse to come.
'How *dare* you call me pig?!' was her shrill cry,
A sin which he has steadily denied
For over forty years now. All the same,
He got the strap next day. I still feel shame
At siding with her version of events
When asked if I'd confirm what he had said.
I knew it wasn't 'pig'- that made no sense -
But let him take her wrath, and crept to bed.

Box Three, Spool Five

When I rewind the tapes of childhood now,
The curt intrusions of my father's grammar,
Correcting almost everything we said,
Have in the intervening years somehow
Become distortions. Why he had to tamper
With our tender syntax, while he led
Us safely, carefully home, I cannot guess,
Or parsed our small affections. Nevertheless,
I don't resent this grammar-laden life,
However much his tense, imperfect rule
Of obstinate corrections spoils the trove
Of childhood memories. That is why this spool,
This tape itself is precious. Loud and clear,
Beneath the surface noise, his love is there.

Writing

My first idea of 'writing' came from him:
'Be quiet, boys, your father's doing his *writing*'.
The dining room a haven, hushed and formal,
A massive order-book and fountain pen,
The flourish of his signature. And then
The rite was over. He'd resume his normal
Self – a salesman, someone less exciting
Than the artist I'd imagined. But within
The folds of this remembrance something serves
To usher in the moment I was smitten:
The dishes done, the kids in bed/ My nerves
All jangling in my head, my mum had written,
In slanting, wispy blue. This fragile verse
Eclipsed my father's writing nonetheless.

Proper Nouns

Grundig, Acromycin, Scraddy-um
Meant 'tape-recorder', 'doctor', 'growing pains',
The private lexicon of family life:
We'd ask 'when will the Acromycin come?
Tell him I can't breathe!' Or infant games,
When 'Scraddy-um!' meant jubilant respite
From tension in our fingers when we squeezed them,
As if those made-up words themselves could ease them.

But 'Grundig' meant the ghosts in our machine
That stored the voice of relatives never seen
From Canada, from the grave, from yesterday:
The outer reaches of our Milky Way.
Those spirit voices sang with stranger sounds
Than the music *we* invented. Proper nouns.

Strictly Private

Like an old radio, the memory, warming up,
Comes alive to dormant, family phrases
Unspoken now for decades, like *the wireless*,
Or private, uncollected nouns like *Gup*,
That narrow-mouthed block of sound so tireless
In fending off affection.
                         There are places
The heart reserves for childhood: not for this.
If I asked you what *Gup* meant, you'd never guess.

But still, it was as real as any word
Collected in the dictionaries, heard
And used and felt a hundred times a day.
Now it sleeps, as words sleep, like the dead,
Its meaning decent by being left unsaid.
Did it render love? I cannot say.

Pray for the Wanderer

Graces, salutations, Marian tropes
We patiently recited day and night.
A blend of high-toned syntax, childlike hopes:
Hail, Holy Queen, To Thee do we cry,
To Thee do we send up our sizes, morning and evening
(No 'mourning', no 'weeping', no 'sighs' in our valley of tears).
We adapted those woeful laments to a prayer more in keeping
With the world as we knew it, remote from such grandiose cares.

But not remote from Heaven: we all felt
The absolute proximity of that place
To every pulse and doubtful thought which dwelt
Within our secret selves. What child could face
That undiscovered country without prayer
Or fail to *pray for the wanderer* who went there?

Vestments

My copes and chasubles, silken stoles and furs,
My surplices edged with lace, were made of sheets
And tea-towels. In my chaste composure, pure
Imagination consecrated sweets
In a ciborium made of precious gold
Or yellow plastic – I was seven years old.
I loved, with sensual sureness, God's great power,
His feminine compensations. This turned sour
When Christmas came and Santa raised his head:
I'd asked for real vestments, but instead
I got a policeman's outfit. '*Priest* and *Police*'
My parents said, 'he must have been confused'.
I prudently agreed, but disabused
Of God and Santa both, my masses ceased.

Dead Languages

The tide of Latin ebbed against my boyhood,
I loved its purple ceremony of sound.
'You *must* bend down like *mice*,' the teacher told us,
'And beat your breast like *so*, eyes to the ground'.
We learnt the rite by ear and loose translation,
But chiefly through its pulse and musical curve
Acquired by means of English simulations
In which the sound and not the sense would serve:
Mea maxima culpa was 'I'm a Mexican cowboy,'
Which made us laugh, but drove the rhythm home.
In Church, the priest intoned and we responded,
A plausible exchange beneath the dome
Which suddenly, after centuries of being heard,
Was stilled by the vernacular absurd.

AZH 402

Anglia, Consul, Zephyr, Hillman Hunter:
Imperial, Roman, Grecian, fabled names
Of modest family cars that mapped my childhood
And still divide those years which memory frames
According to the car that drove or idled
While family life progressed or came asunder.
'I think we had the Consul then', we say
As if to verify some childish fray
Which idles like an engine as we muse
On what went wrong, on whom we should accuse.
A car door slams, the past is out of reach,
The Hillman Hunter roars across the beach
And leaves the memory stranded, far behind:
Those epic names remain, truth of a kind.

Bardolino

'Bardolino' was the word I borrowed
From the bottle of wine my parents drank on Sunday.
I loved its comical, concertina-sound,
Its flavoured surge of vowels my private code
For happiness: a childlike chant unsorrowed
By experience, the wine-dark gloom that one day
Would lie behind these sounds, as when I found
Myself *in* Bardolino. She first showed
Her Mediterranean splendour, and the word
Acquired for me, at last, its primary meaning:
An affluent haven of streets and vistas seeming
To confirm that childhood mantra I'd procured.
But my Italian summer was to fade
And lose possession of the word I'd made.

A Musical Life

My Uncle Reggie sang the sweetest song.
At Christmas parties, musical soirées,
His tenor voice would soar. A murmuring throng
Of friends and relatives, silenced by the strains
Of Percy French, *The Woods of Gortnamona*,
Would egg him on for more: *Bravo! Ancora!*
It's true: all music was his grave delight,
But never his profession, try as he might
To break the spell of hardship which ensnared him
In ill-paid work. No talent had prepared him
For the fatal strain of trying to make his living.
At our wedding, when he'd finished singing,
'You never lost it, Reggie!,' someone cried.
'Ah, indeed I did,' he said, and sighed.

My Remarkable Uncle

Uncle Bill is crossing Porter's Field
In a rented car crowded with jubilant kids
Who fall around with laughter as he feigns
A heart attack, collapsing on the wheel.
His wayward steering, simulated chest pains
And long, exhausted sighs increase our bids
For terror: 'die again!' He swerves the car.
It lurches, stops in 1972.

That August evening, propping up the bar
In Murray's pub in Lusk he takes the view
That life in Canada ('What's it *really* like?')
Is 'way too serious…still, for the children's sake….'
He's going back. To ice-flows, grizzly bears.
Or some such fable. No-one really cares.

Something Blue from the Pines

The compact double-bed was lowered down.
I could not see, but heard behind the curtain
Which screened them off from us when bedtime came,
How it sighed and thumped onto the floor.
The scrape of folding metal chairs would follow.
Shuffles. Murmurs. Vesperal baritone,
My mother's calm response. My father's snore.
The caravan swaying slightly. The wind from the shore.

This all came back in 1981
With *Something Blue*: a half-remembered song
In some Canadian wilderness called 'The Pines'.
By then those childhood summers had been long
Eclipsed and ruined. Family life instead
Lay cold and voided, like an unmade bed.

Intolerance

Where is Sister Maria Teresa now?
That bony, shrill, misguided, stiff-hemmed bridesmaid,
Who 'prayed for the reconciliation of two dear friends',
Or Father H-, the laughing priest of my childhood,
That red-faced dandler. In Heaven making amends
For his sinister, mad obedience? I don't know.
I cannot condemn or forgive – they were slaves of that
Church
Which governed my parents and left them both in the lurch.

Why should I lacerate a foolish nun
Or even a treacherous, unforgiving priest,
Now that their reckless servitude is done?
We have other demons now, to say the least:
Purple or paled-faced, the bullies still remain,
Ordained as *line managers*, and just as insane.

A War Miniature

To Miss Cecily Allen. From Richard O'Reilly. November 21st, 1917

Papa O'Reilly's first-born, favourite son
Sat for the Crown Exams, was sent to London.
'Dear Father', he wrote from Heywards, 'all is well,
Our rooms are vast and sunlit! You can tell
The Dublin men like me from all the rest:
Church-going, homesick, on for a laugh, hard pressed
To understand this war against the Hun.
Greet Mamma for me. Ever, your loving son'.

This was my great-uncle Richard, more-or-less,
Until some girl left a feather upon his desk
And shamed him stupidly into the mud and pain,
Dreaming of her and of Canada. All in vain:
His postcard reached her empty hands too late
And left his undone father disconsolate.

The Nature of Things

My sheets were soaked in urine every morning
Despite cajolements, warnings, extreme thirst:
Then rubber sheets, the stink of piss, a wearing
Shame on holidays, in hospitals. The worst
Was when the shrill-voiced matron loudly asked
Who was the cat who wet the bed? This masked
Her ignorance, mother tried to reassure me,
And then, a salesman told her he could cure me.

In six weeks, I was cured. The bed stayed dry -
A metal sheet attached to an alarm
Which woke me when I peed. This meant that I
Soon slept straight through, encouraged by the charm
Of letters from the salesman.   His firm ailed:
Undone by too much kindness, it soon failed.

The Music Makers

Piano lessons: white keys, black keys, staves,
A vast, domestic Upright, varnished black
With *Serma* on the lid. Our music case,
Its grip secured with steel, a leather bag
Whose shape proclaimed its purpose. Once a week
With gentle Miss McKenzie, we would seek
Our scuffed and dog-eared music from its depths
And stumble through the grammar: scales and clefs.

We were never very good, but we persisted,
Obedient to my father, who insisted
His organ teacher solemnly foretold
Our special gift when we were just days' old.
And so the die was cast for John and me,
The music makers of the family.

The Back Gardens

In memory of F.G.

Long, lush gardens bordered with low walls,
A clutch of apple trees we called 'the orchard',
A sandpit sunk in stone. Those white-sleeved children
Absorbed in safe imaginings, playing there:
The long back gardens.
                         'Frances!' someone calls,
'You're wanted for your tea!': the girl feels awkward,
The switch from 'nurse' to child is much too sudden
For wounded Cowboys and Indians in her care.

She drifts away in fading summer light
Across the gardens and the years. That night
She was pastoral, lovely, safe, and ten years old.

I cannot keep her there. It must be told:
Her white-faced children, an ambulance, the rain,
A nurse assuring them that she felt no pain.

Bucket and Spade

The slather of cold cream on burning arms
And reddened legs, the timid lap of water
Ebbing skin and seaweed: these are preludes
To an infant afternoon of dreams in sand
Which binds that tiny figure on the beach
To a future where the deckchairs are forlorn.
The tide of sixty years has not outworn
The rites of bucket and spade, nor can it breach
The privacy of those dreams. Beyond a bland
Remembrance ('holiday snaps'), this rapture moves
And reawakens in a son or daughter,
Not every generation, but no harm:
In 1929 and '91,
My father felt it first, and then my son.

The Rider

When I was seven, a Honda, braking hard,
Shrieked and skidded, and broke my collar-bone:
I'd dashed across the road on my way home
And fell beneath the wheel.
                                  How easily
I moved those motorbikes across the yard
When I was twelve: *Suzuki, Kawasaki,*
Those euphonies of steel and gleaming chrome
Were still enough to crush a kid like me,
But now I knew the downward push and pull,
The leverage and balance which were needed
To mount them safely.
                                Had it been my skull,
And not my shoulder, when that bike, unheeded,
Collided with my seven years, what then?
Oh blameless rider, brake for me again.

Captain Extra Mild

Cigarettes were safe and stylish then,
And Captain Extra Mild was there to prove it:
His gleaming bands of gold on navy serge,
His dazzling cuff, his braided cap, alluded
To some privileged region we had never seen
Except within the Sunday magazine
Which graced the sober news-sheets every week
With gusto: sexual *senior-service* chic.

We never saw his face. But we could guess
At his demeanour in the Officers' Mess,
The smiling, tanned supremacy of his life,
His debonair cigarettes, his scented wife.
He disappeared one day into the hills
And in his place a warning: *smoking kills.*

Notices

I hoisted the window-grilles at six each evening,
And let them sag with an iron clatter each day
To announce the start of business on Emmet Road.
Summer work in my father's shop: a way
Of keeping the 'tedious, limping hours at bay'
Inscribed in my mother's blue-bound *Oscar Wilde*.
Televisions, motorbikes, the sundry growth of a business
He'd hardly begun, when he was on the road:
You can rely on Pye. The gleaming wetness
Of washed concrete. 'Spare parts'. *For Sale* and *Sold*
In vivid, felt-tipped red. Old catalogues piled
In stacks of no importance. Customers reading
The new notices, inscribed in earnest blue:
Join our Christmas Club! A forming queue.

School-going

Galloping past the houses after lunch
To catch the bus for school, I'd gasp, and urge
My brother to keep up: 'it's twenty past!'
But asthma made him slow – 'you're going too fast!'
The schoolbags on our backs would spur us on,
Their slap and jostle hurried us along
The sloping concrete. I would strain to hear
The engine's iron shudder.
                              'Nearly there!'
I'd call to John, the bus-stop within reach,
His wheezing frame behind. Then I'd stretch
And yank him forward, frantic for the bus
To loom and slow, and board both of us.

This is the oldest story in the world
Of rescue, then regret: of something spoiled.

Junior Infants

Miss Dawson was a vixen with a cane,
Glamorous-strict, peremptory in high heels,
Sexual-doctrinaire. Reward and pain,
The natural compass points of her appeal
To order. 'Infant' boys, aged five, we'd yearn
To win her cool approval, soft and stern.
Her blonde interrogations, hands on hips,
The voice of Church and State from full-glossed lips.
A vital contradiction, it now seems,
Of frumpy nuns, those red-faced priests, the reams
Of catholic-nationalist dogma we'd receive
From her and other teachers. Who'd believe
That half a century later, I can summon
This thrilling mediatrix? What a woman.

The Conventions

Coleman, White, O'Connor, Ryan, Chrystal.
Surnames were the modal norm in school,
And uniforms in 'charcoal grey' and purple,
With tightly beaded stitching on the sleeve
And cap. The seniors, larking in the yard,
Wore black with darts of gold. The swish and frock
Of whispering soutanes and tasselled cinctures
Hoisted by the Brothers while they strode
Or strutted there, with peeping slits that showed
Their legs beneath, like first names hid from view
On shy occasions, spoke against those bleak,
Arrested courtesies which held in check
The dangerous progressions they might know
In *Brian, Harry, Aidan, Lorcan, Joe.*

Night Prayers

I stifled fear in the long dark corridor
Swelling with boys. We moved on that first night
Hastened by baying prefects, waving torches,
Into the chapel drenched in harsh blunt light.
Those familiar with the drone began:
Litany of order, time-accustomed cant.
I knelt on wood beside my brother John,
Riveted by this wailing, boyish descant.

Brothers were given rooms. I closed the door
Against the wooden dread of that whole evening
And afterwards lay in bed, half-praying, half-dreaming,
As darkness gulfed the room. Then it came clear:
My head full with that brilliant September day
And my parents leaving, leaving, leaving.

Sunday Mass

A strident celibate warms to his dreadful theme.
Our heads are lowered; some of us want to laugh
At his morbid purity: *filthy, dirty, clean,*
Hysterical keywords streaming through the sun
Like particles on this sterile winter morning.
The college chapel heaves with hymns to tedium
And barren, varnished piety. Then it's done:
The sepia-stale emission. Servile yearning.

Who could guess in the seventies where this was going?
– The Marian-blue guitar, the sexless swaying,
The simple-minded rapture, or the cloying
Three-chord, popsong ecstasy of knowing
That Jesus was alive and celibate still,
Though watered down, or idolized at will.

Radio Sounds

This happened every night in school, this close
Of play: I'd pull the woollen blanket round
My face, and listen for my brother's muffled lifeline
Of radio sounds, a world beyond the drab,
Discoloured silences and mild assaults
And summary confiscations we endured.
His bed so close to mine. I was inured,
Or so I thought, to all those schoolboy taunts
Which plagued his sleep. Not mine. The comforting blab
Of Late Night Extra soothed him through the night.
But first he'd turn it off, because the sound
Kept me awake. And then back on. He'd pause
And listen to me sleeping, unaware,
As I sank down, and he came up for air.

Avenues

The Front Walks on Sunday afternoons
Where 'sitting room' took place in crouching cars,
On tarmac slopes before the school, are avenues.
The parents huddled there with silent sons
Are gone. The avenues remain, and lead
To sad retrievals in the kissing seat,
The furtive, cramped Fiesta of my father,
Or of myself.
          When I got straightened out
And found a place to live, I joked about
The 'sad Dads in McDonald's', curbed the pain
Of weekly separations, once again.
Boarded, then divorced. Well, no great matter:
Families often fade or fall apart,
But love persists, re-groups, survives. Take heart.

Fathers and Sons

You used to say that I was at my best
Just rocking Fiachra gently while he slept,
A patient trance of motion on the crest
Of sleep. The sunlit garden where we kept
This father-son communion every day
Preserved by you in memory. Hard to say
How much this tender sequence kept us going
In darker times. There's just no way of knowing.

But what I know is this, now he's full grown,
And I see younger fathers with their sons
Absorbed and intimate, happy on their own,
Intent upon each other, this returns:
The infant-fingered happiness anew
Of fatherhood. And this I owe to you.

In Herbert Park

A weekend father angrily chides his son:
An upturned, tear-stained face beseeching mine,
His fingers clutch my sleeve as I bend down
To reason with him for the *umpteenth* time
That throwing stones at ducks is simply *wrong*.
He wails remorse and begs me, *don't tell mom.*
By now, we're holding hands. Then, unaware,
We're photographed by someone standing there,
A family friend, who'd watched the scene unfold
And captured this: the vanishing point, untold,
In which our love commingled. Even now,
Considering that photograph, somehow
Its fragile grace and pain I still prefer
To beaming family portraits, free from care.

Swimming Lessons

The shriek of whistles. Flesh on wet, green tiles.
Those shivering Sunday mornings, full of dread
And skinny cowardice. Down the bobbing aisles
That separate real swimmers from the herd
Of panicked children gulping in the shallows,
I see my younger brother, unafraid.
He holds his nose, jumps in. There's nothing callow
About his strong, clean strokes, no fear betrayed.

Timid, aquaphobic boys like me
Who hate the chlorine, mortally dread the sea,
Acquire a taste for fear, and what they learn
Is death-rehearsal, over and over again.
Wakened by soft voices, you will drown:
These are useless lessons, put them down.

Lost Things

Anyone who's parented might shun
Those beating wings and burning towers, have done
With all such Greek beseechments (rape, the swan,
The girl), leave these alone, or stumble on
Through reverenced rubbish, centuries of cant,
The gong-tormented *Angelus*, the chant
Of punishment, obedience and the fruit
Of fallen bed-time stories.
                      Now the brute
Disclosures come. The slouching beast is bayed,
Exposed, disgraced. But suddenly he's re-made,
And threatens retribution everywhere
As Eastern icons in the scorching air
Confirm that what was lost has now been found,
And topless towers burn right down to the ground.

A Loanword

Among his calm deliveries – infant coinage-,
Babash, meaning 'blanket', stayed the course
While other words grew up or fell away.
We both adapted to its Slavic sound,
Adopted its 'Hungarian' tang, and found
It vital (frantic searches: *Where's the Babash?*).
Borrowed, yellow, woollen, edged with silk,
It covered him at first, and then it shrank.
As he grew up and it grew smaller still
Between his fingers, comforting him until
He'd swiftly hide it when his friends appeared,
The word at last was gone.
                      We're not prepared
To think of love as something that's on loan,
Though he's in Hungary now, and fully grown.

A Farm Visit

The sullen farmer crunched across the gravel
And gestured us within. Croatian small-talk,
While we waited for the cheese. His nod to me,
The quizzical grappa and glasses in his hand:
That much was something I could understand.
I gulped the burning liquid in relief,
And took in trophies, a sideboard, his reticent wife.
Then talk (I was told) of a son in medical school.
A sudden cloudburst broke through their conversation
Which made it imperative. Stanislav's translation:
The fields round here are covered still with mines
Left by the Serbs, disguised as children's toys.
Which made me think of Dara in my bloodied arms
After an accident. Racing for help through his cries.

The Girl in the Frame

Before she was *Nana*, before she was married to Jack,
Before those stern encumbrances framed her life,
She was the girl my father now keeps by his bed,
Impossibly fresh as all youth. Her clever mouth,
Magnificent eyes and selfishly-perfect hair,
Her *warmth*, her comely happiness is there.
She contradicts everything she became:
This spirited, almost wanton girl in the frame.
She could never have guessed at the matriarch she would become,
At the hardening years which stiffened her natural bloom,
And formed her drastic piety. Perhaps there were some
Who knew her better, who still could feel the charm
Which animates that photo. It, for once,
Releases this girl from *Nana* and from us.

The Men Who Left

Mr Phelan was the first to go:
His tall frame lapsed. One night, he slipped away
And left his iron-voiced, squawking wife alone.
Then Mr Cheevers: paunch, moustache, the glow
Of a fat cigar. We knew he'd never stay,
The women said. She's better on her own.
Fictive, hushed departures. Where had they gone?
To England, mostly, someone said, or Spain.

We washed away those absences, but then
A harrowing, third departure made them real.
Before he went, a sit-down, family trial:
Indictments, shamings in the exhausted kitchen.
His head bent low, my mother harsh and pale,
The unmistakable sound of a rending veil.

Messages

'Messages' for us meant 'groceries', parcels of meat
Reposed in the tabernacle-fridge overnight
And often attached to a gerund, like *drying the delph*
Or *going for the messages*. You could feel the weight
Of those compact, processional anchors through the day:
Bread-man, meat-man, milk-man, till Daddy came home
With evening treats in his pocket and something to say.
The perfect cadencer. *Sweet-man.* Arbiter. Firm.

Secure in his judgments, we fell fast asleep
Until blood in those loosening parcels began to seep
And 'messages' came to mean, sooner or later,
Stained evasions attached to a refrigerator.
Decades later, the word joins up with 'text'
And re-attaches itself to whatever's next.

Wedding Photos

His morning suit with tails, her wedding gown,
Disposed in silken circles on the lawn.
My youthful parents, their idea of heaven:
A Dublin hotel in 1957.
The monochrome perfection of it all,
A nuptial Eden, innocent of the Fall.
Embossed and bound with stiffened, white-rosed paper,
Their wedding album, slip-cased, tissue-leaved,
Preserves those radiant images which later
Were traduced, their virgin grace bereaved
By something inborn, natural, long suppressed.
Those photos were exposed, not much is left.
That lustrous bride and groom, do not dismay them:
They smile into a future that betrayed them.

Notes and Acknowledgements

Polite Forms was written between January, 2008 and June, 2011. Although the whole sequence is, perhaps self-evidently, a meditation on family life written from the perspective of a man in his early fifties, one of the poems, which I am inclined not to identify here, was written as far back as 1984, when I was twenty-six years old. It was published, in a slightly different form, in *Acta Victoriana*, a journal which issues from Victoria College in the University of Toronto. *Acta* used to advertise itself as 'Canada's oldest literary periodical', a claim which for some reason has always given me great pleasure. In those days (the early 1980s), the University of Toronto published several journals of poetry and prose, all of them immaculately edited and handsomely produced, which were expressly intended to encourage the work of staff and students lucky enough to be part of that remarkable institution. I recall the appearance of Northrop Frye, Kathleen Coburn and Aubrey Rosenberg (among others) in those journals cheek by jowl with the very first work by graduate students such as myself. In any case, the reason I draw attention to this unnamed poem, which appears in a revised version here, is that my twin brother John liked the original so much that he framed and displayed it when he worked as a teacher, conductor and theatre director in Mullingar (near where I now live). That was over twenty-five years ago, but I have always been immensely grateful for the fact that so many people read that poem on John's kitchen wall and enjoyed it. The material expression of my gratitude lies in these poems which really do originate in that domestically-displayed lyric, even if it is unlikely that I could have written the remainder of *Polite Forms* much sooner than I did. John has my heartfelt thanks for having shared that poem with other people, just as I am grateful to *Acta Victoriana* for having published it in the first place. It has waited all these years to join its undoubted companions in this collection.

There are many others whom I must thank. Declan Kiberd, whose kindness as a friend and colleague is only rivalled by his lustre and brilliance as a critic and writer, read these poems with a degree of empathy and encouragement that materially influenced my decision to publish them. Roy Foster, likewise, accepted my importunities with forgiving grace, was hugely helpful in his response to my work and offered many suggestions which improved my own efforts to close the gap between memoir and poetic utterance. Jaime Jones, Frank Lawrence and Maria Patricia O'Connor were characteristically positive and responsive when I asked them to read some of these poems, as were Porscha Fermanis (who offered a decisive comment at a difficult moment) and Robert Gerwarth, who is the most serenely encouraging of close friends.

I find it difficult to express the extent of my immense debt to Eithne Graham, who knows the territory which *Polite Forms* surveys better than anyone (other than myself), for having read these poems and commented on them as they emerged. It is a great pleasure to thank Karina Daly, who read early drafts of these poems with such gratifying enthusiasm. To Lorraine Byrne Bodley I express heartfelt thanks for her cherished support and crucial assistance. I also thank Dan Farrelly and Lilian Chambers of Carysfort Press for having shown such alacrity, expertise and kindness in their care of my work. My dearest wife Xiao Mei, in faraway China as I thank her here, created and nurtured the environment in which I am so fortunate to live and write.

When I mustered the courage (or the impertinence) to ask Seamus Heaney to read these poems, I could not have anticipated the sheer generosity and detail of his response. To have had the benefit of his close reading is a singular privilege that speaks for itself, and I am deeply grateful for it. His recommendations as to technique and his aesthetic commentary were a stimulus to revision that I feel incredibly lucky to have received.

My final acknowledgement of thanks returns me to Toronto, where in the summer of 2009 I met the Canadian poet and literary scholar Chantel Lavoie. I hope it is sufficient to remark that her reception of my work (in progress as it then was) proved vital to its final outcome, and that she became the kind of ideal reader (and literary editor) one hopes for but rarely encounters.

Polite Forms is dedicated to my sons, Fiachra and Dara. I ardently hope they will enjoy it, but I am not shy to add that there is a world of difference between lived experience (theirs, mine) and the public representations which poetry affords. With that muted *caveat lector* I close this family album and hope for the best.

Harry White
Legan, 2011